Nature Trails in Northamptonshire

Mia Butler

*For my friend John Elliott,
who cares for the countryside and all its creatures.*

Front Cover: Summer Leys Nature Reserve

Previous titles by the same author
Northamptonshire Rambles	Countryside Books 1991
Exploring the Nene Way	Countryside Books 1992
Let's Go Walkabout in Northamptonshire	R. Wharton 1996
Secrets & Treasures of Northamptonshire	S.B. Publications 1996
A Northamptonshire Quiz Book	S.B. Publications 1997
Walks in Mysterious Northamptonshire (with Marian Pipe)	Sigma Press 1999
Learn Yersalf Northamptonshire Dialect (with Colin Eaton)	Nostalgia Publications 1999
Second Northamptonshire Quiz Book (with Colin Eaton)	S.B. Publications 2000

Copyright © 2002 Mia Butler
All rights reserved. No part of this publication may be reproduced, in any form or by any means, without the prior consent of the author.

Published by John Nickalls Publications
ISBN: 1 904136 03 6

Printed by Geo. R. Reeve Ltd.
9-11 Town Green, Wymondham, Norfolk, NR18 0BD

ACKNOWLEDGEMENTS

My sincere appreciation is due to many friends and colleagues who have kindly shown an interest in my efforts and given freely of their support and knowledge – they will recognise themselves, I feel sure. Particular greetings and thanks must be showered upon close friends, such as Marian Pipe, for her splendid renderings of the walks in her maps. Also to Colin Eaton who has given unstinting assistance and executed the (impossible to me) task of transferring the text onto disc. A number of photographs have been kindly loaned to me for this project, by lovers of the countryside, these include Cliff Christie, Colin Eaton, John Elliott, Ralph Mitchell, Ioan Thomas, Dr G. W. Thompson, The Wildlife Trust and some are by the author.

Mia Butler

CONTENTS

1	Collyweston Quarries Nature Reserve and environs.	1
2	Farthinghoe Local Nature Reserve with Little and Great Purston.	6
3	Finedon Pocket Park and Cally Banks Nature Reserve.	11
4	Glapthorn Cow Pastures and Short Wood Nature Reserves.	18
5	Gretton and Paddock Park.	23
6	Islip and Titchmarsh Local Nature Reserve.	29
7	Kinewell Lake Nature Reserve and environs.	35
8	Pitsford Water and Nature Reserve.	42
9	Stoke Bruerne and Nature Reserve.	48
10	Stoke Wood End Quarter and environs.	53
11	Summer Leys Local Nature Reserve and Great Doddington.	60
12	Twywell Hills and Dales and Twywell.	66

INTRODUCTION

Do you sometimes crave an amble under an infinite blue sky, over an endless rolling landscape, with tufty grass unfurling like a wide ribbon beneath your feet? To be far away from the mad antics of the motorist, the ugly possibility of pent-up aggression and instead, let the country air fill the lungs and revitalise? Is there a sentinel church spire peeping over ancient trees in a tiny cluster of a hamlet tucked into far acres, that signals freedom for mind and body?

Wander into the stillness of the green wood, where only birdsong breaks the silence, or the soft rustle in the grass tells of unseen life. Under the lacy canopy, that other bustling world soon disappears. Listen to the silence, where maybe a swift fallow deer will cross the path and the shy denizens of the undergrowth maybe observing you, as they scratch and search among the leafy litter, where crab apples and acorns are a feast for many.

Stroll in the cool glades, on the spinney's edge, or the swathes of hills and hollows. The tiny, shy dormouse with bright eyes might be on his aerial travels among the honeysuckle vines. Observe an isolated badger sett, to perhaps return at dusk to watch, at a respectful distance, these nocturnal families rummaging for their sustenance.

Stand still and silent, to sniff at the earthy smells, like the odour of the fox, to detect delicate nuances of that secret undergrowth world and be aware of movement in fresh molehills as the velvety creatures are busy in the labrynth of tunnels.

See the imprint of a dainty hoof, the intricate gossamer thread of the spider's web and the powder-puff white tails of the rabbits with twitchy noses.

In the early summer, colour carpets our woods with bluebells and butterflies galore flit in and out of the dapples. Damselflies and dragonflies hunt and hover in damp places. Listen for the high-flying lark, the cheeky cuckoo, and in the cool of the evening, the elusive nightingale.

A tapping on wood and the shrill yaffle identifies the smart woodpecker, as the treecreeper and nuthatch spiral up and down the tree trunks in their constant search for insects.

Appreciate the swans on the river, trailed by grey signets as big as their parents. Coots and ducks with strings of tiny balls of fluff madly paddling to keep up.

One could go on in this vein for ever, but the message is – ENJOY.

WALK 1

THE DEEPS NATURE RESERVE AND COLLYWESTON
Distance 4 miles
Map OS Landranger 141. 1:50 000
Grid ref: SP005036
Nearest town – Stamford

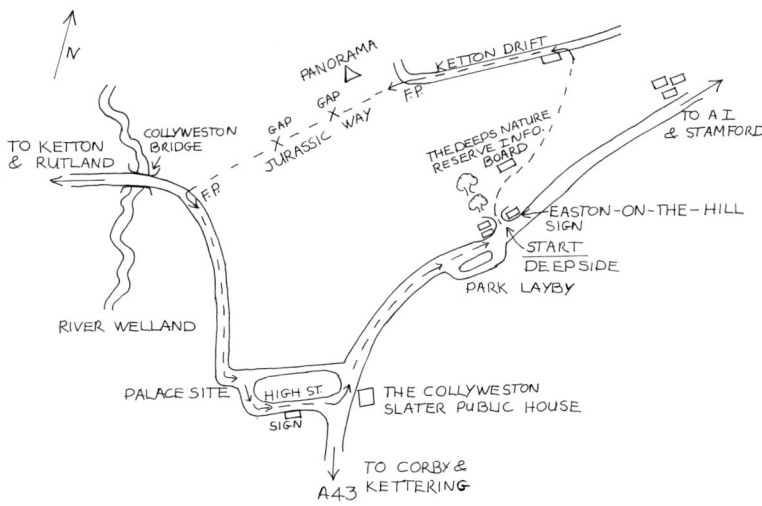

Start on the A43 Kettering to Stamford road, going north, initially passing through Collyweston on a fairly open stretch. Watch for the sign for Easton-on-the-Hill on the left verge, with a spacious layby opposite for parking.

A scattering of houses lie back on a private road, Deep Side, so please observe the notices before entering the reserve, commonly known as The Deeps.

This is a rocky, hilly area, now totally colonised and has interesting segments of walls and remnants of Collyweston stone which were quarried here until 1960, for the production of slates. Such rooftops are still evident today, not only in the immediate district, but all over the county. The stone was left exposed to the elements, as nature took its course, when heavy winter frosts caused the blocks to split into thin sheets. There was even a plan, at one time, it is rumoured, to create a massive 'deep freeze' unit to do the same job!

An interesting article lists almost thirty names of Collyweston slate sizes, given to Sir David Scott by Mr Knapp of that village. These intriguing measures include such names as:- Outrills, Even and Large Mumfits, Imbos, Outbos and Whippets.

WALK

Enter the reserve through the kissing-gate and note the Information Board, then take the designated path, going away from the main road over some rough terrain, to exit on the far side by two gates into the open playing field. Head for the clutch of huts in the far corner, passing through the gap in the hedge to join the Jurassic Way on the Ketton Drift track.

One cannot fail to be entranced with the splendour of the valley, where the wooded slopes lend both substance and colour regardless of season.

Bear left to where the lane curves off down the hill. Instead, go forward over the stile and three fields to planks over the ditch at the road to Ketton. Collyweston bridge, of medieval origin, with six arches, spans the River Welland, the boundary between Northamptonshire and England's smallest county, Rutland.

Collyweston Bridge over River Welland

Start up toward Collyweston on the quiet road, which becomes steep and protracted, but well worth the effort.

This delectable village is laced with history. At the top of the hill facing, is a stone wall, a palace site, the early residence of Lord Cromwell, Treasurer to King Henry VI. Later, in 1486, to become the home of Lady Margaret Beaufort, Countess of Richmond and mother of Henry VII, the monarch who was to conclude the Wars of the Roses and instigate the Tudor dynasty.

Follow the wall to turn left where elegant houses line the wide thoroughfare in the High Street. A lofty sign reflects the local tradition of the specialist slater, for which the place is noted.

Left at the main road, with the Collyweston Slater public house on the far side. Stay on the pavement set back from the highway to return to Deep Side.

Ketton Drift Collyweston Stone Wall

COLLYWESTON QUARRIES NATURE RESERVE

Known locally as The Deeps, this singular quarry site of 19 acres once yielded the famous Collyweston slate renowned throughout the land. Closed down for some years, the grey-blue slates are easily recognisable in the surrounding villages and further afield. The semi-natural limestone grassland qualifies as an SSSI (Site of Special Scientific Interest).

Such areas now being rare, where motorbike scrambling had previously caused damage, The Wildlife Trust took over the site management in 1983, with permission of the local Parish Council and Burghley Estates, in order to restore the land by scrub removal and winter grazing by sheep.

Consequently, the improvement of limestone vegetation has encouraged growth appropriate to the content and displays in its sandy soil, tussocks of torgrass and brome, according to season.

Keen grazing both by sheep and rabbits, have given rise to 200 species of wildflower and 2 parasitic plants, knapweed broomrake and common dodder, now frequent, may be found from May to August.

The most bright flowering time is early July, with the blooms of dyer's green weed, whose blossoms were once used to make yellow dye. Toadstools too, flourish in this environment.

Shrub includes blackberry and hawthorn, interspersed with privet and wild rose among oaks and planted apple trees.

Marsh Marigolds

Insects such as small heath, gatekeeper butterflies and burnet moths thrive, feasting on knapweed. It is a sanctuary for the rare glow-worm, in addition to the ant and grasshopper, bees and bugs galore.

Watch for the cheeky jay, whitethroat and skylark, soaring far above and over the slopes of the Welland Valley.

PLACES OF INTEREST

WAKERLEY GREAT WOOD

Wakerley Great Wood, one of the larger tracts of Rockingham Forest, situated on the west side of the A43, is managed by Forest Enterprise, whose office is at Top Lodge, Fineshade, on the far side of that road.

In medieval times, the two hundred square miles of the forest gave shelter to hamlets, farms and open land for grazing animals. It was considered to be sacrosanct, purely for royal hunting forays and specifically 'for the monarch's pleasure', when the illegal killing of a deer resulted in the penalty of death.

Now classified as six hundred acres of ancient woodland, Wakerley Wood enfolds a diversity of flora and fauna, offering shady walks, orienteering, cycling, horse riding, picnic sites, car parking and toilet facilities, throughout the year.

PRIEST'S HOUSE, EASTON ON THE HILL

Dating from the late 15th century, this compact and rare edifice was thought to have been erected to serve as a residence for the clergy.

Built of local stone with a roof of Collyweston slate, it has an upstairs room with a fireplace and a timber roof and is now in use as a limited museum.

Saved from demolition in the 20th century, it was purchased and restored by the National Trust, where the ground floor may have more recently been utilized as a stable prior to the later function as a meeting room.

WALK 2

FARTHINGHOE LOCAL NATURE RESERVE
Distance 3 miles
Map OS Landranger 151. 1:50 000
Grid ref: SP518404
Nearest town – Brackley

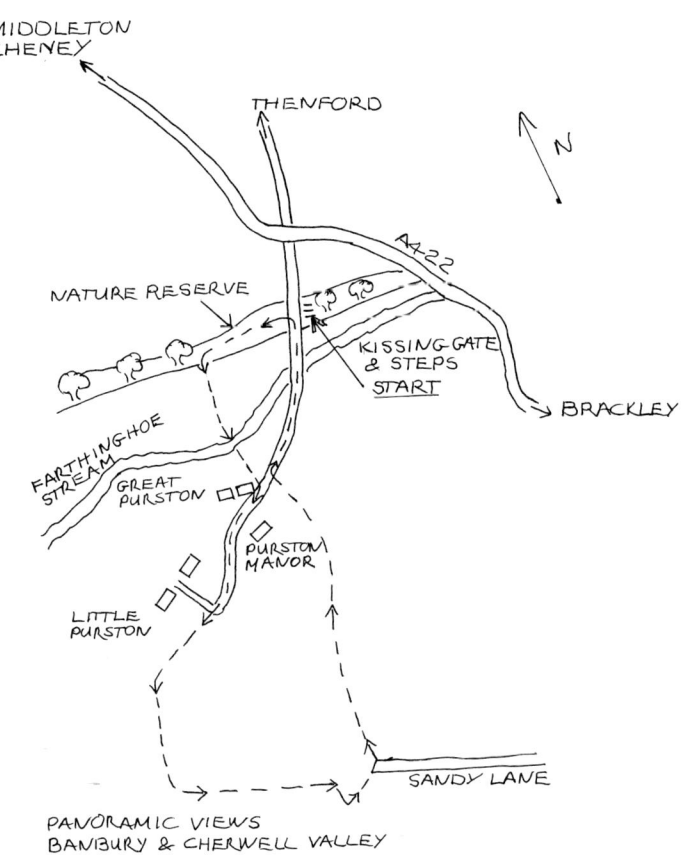

Almost at the southern-most tip of the county, this charming area of countryside, reflected in the hills and meadows, manages to hang on to the much-loved cowslips, when many are being sacrificed to modern farming methods.

Largely unaffected by human activity since the closure of the railway line, and later the landfill site, plants thriving on disturbed soil have made good and now, having responded favourably, more cover has been established.

WALK

Park on the bridge at the entrance to the reserve with care.

Enter the reserve through the kissing-gate, going immediately down the steps, to turn left to follow the path to the fence at the western end. Here, views across the brook valley ahead are toward Great Purston on the hill, where the church steeple at Middleton Cheney shows to the north-west.

Climb over the post and rail fence and turn sharp left over an old railway stile, to continue on the footpath down to the small lake at the bottom of the hill. Coot, moorhen, little grebe and other water birds evidently find this a convenient nesting-site.

Farthinghoe Walk Vista

Over the meadow a footbridge spans Farthinghoe Stream (or Purston Brook), as through the gate of the neighbouring pasture, the path rises diagonally to meet the narrow road to Great Purston.

The Old Manor House and dwellings comprising this hamlet are built of local Hornton stone, whose roof tiles are smothered by moss, and the surrounding wall festooned with lichen. The Stud House and stables lie beyond, on the way to Little Purston.

Stay on the quiet road as far as the bend, with a barn on the corner, as the waymark points through the gate to the left to groups of standing trees, then bears toward the hedge and a hunting gate.

A steep pull at an angle now to the highest point of the walk and perhaps a deserved pause to admire the panoramic vista unfurling away to the horizon over to Middleton Cheney and Banbury, in the adjacent county.

At this junction, sharp left along the hedgerow to walk atop the ridge, before dipping gently on the northern slope. A minor kink at the base of the hill precedes the merge into Sandy Lane, which may be muddy in inclement weather conditions.

The path turns 90 degrees to the left on to the bridleway back toward Purston, where several interesting plants thrive beside the old track. Look out for common fleabane, red bartsia, mayweed, knapweed and clover. Further along the hedgerow to the right, pass through the gate between two large oaks. There is a thatched stone barn in the far corner and once over the rise, Purston Manor reappears.

New woodland, planted about five years ago is becoming established and beyond, the ha-ha and Manor are now visible. Go through the gate by the surrounding wall of the orchard, where a spinney tucked in the fold of the land almost obscures Primrose Pool, as the bridleway soon rejoins the lane.

A minor stone bridge heralds the incline to re-enter the reserve.

FARTHINGHOE LOCAL NATURE RESERVE

Declared a local nature reserve in 1993 by Northamptonshire County Council, this park of roughly 4 acres is very successfully managed by dedicated members of The Wildlife Trust. Following the closure of the London and North Western Railway line in 1963, the cutting has since been especially slanted toward producing a rich mix of grass and woodland.

The original meadow, formerly the Waste Recycling Centre, was previously used for the loading of animals bound for Banbury Market. It has, however, responded to careful husbandry in a mowing regime designed to restore knapweed, scabious and the ox-eye daisy, among other species.

The marbled white, mainly found only in the south of the county, partial to the shaggy knapweed, are among the 26 species of butterfly recorded here, alongside the small skipper, which prefer the prickly teasel. Dragonflies and damselflies are numerous and frequently found in their chosen breeding grounds, in the Farthinghoe Stream nearby.

Hawthorn and blackthorn scrub offer shelter, food and nesting-sites for all three woodpecker types, co-habiting with tawny owls, tits, sparrows and the likewise.

Badgers find plenty to forage and mammals include muntjac deer, grey squirrel, rabbit and hare. Smaller species are shrew, vole, woodmouse and some harvest mice.

The infill areas have been planted with alder, birch, cherry, hornbeam, oak, rowan, ash, beech and guelder rose.

Specific paths and handy seats afford fine vistas across the valley to Purston or west, over the Cherwell Valley.

PLACES OF INTEREST
BRACKLEY

Brackley exudes an ambience of genteel tranquility, inviting the visitor to take a leisurely stroll to admire and enjoy the historical background of the old buildings of brick and stone.

The surgence of the wool trade brought prosperity to this charming community, developed from an early Roman settlement, through the Middle Ages and is reflected today in its wide approach on the mile-long, tree-lined main street.

Although the castle was destroyed in 1173, now the elegant Town Hall, erected over the arches by the 1st Duke of Bridgewater in 1706, presents a satisfying centre-piece.

St. James' Chapel, originally built as the Hospital of St. James and St. John, founded in 1150 by the Earl of Leicester, was to become part of Magdalen College School, which gained a considerable reputation of excellence from an early date.

Other pleasing façades, such as the almshouses, founded by Sir Thomas Crewe in 1633 and the old Manor House, are among the attractions of the promenade.

SULGRAVE MANOR

Lawrence Washington, a wool-stapler and Mayor of Northampton, built the Manor, having purchased the estate from Henry VIII in the 16th century. Several generations later, one of his descendants, John Washington, emigrated to Virginia in 1656 and subsequently, George Washington became the first President of the United States.

In 1914 a century of peace was celebrated by the gift of the Manor from British subscribers to the peoples of both countries. Now a popular venue, the house attracts visitors from this country and particularly 'across the pond', as the 'stars and stripes' has a prominent position in the surrounding garden.

Tudor and Queen Anne furnishings, topiary and herb gardens, exhibitions and tours, events and enactments. Also Tudor workshops, giftshop, restaurant and all facilities are available.

WALK 3

FINEDON POCKET PARK AND
CALLY BANKS NATURE RESERVE
Distance 4 miles
Map OS Landranger 141. 1:50 000
Grid ref: SP 910722
Nearest town – Finedon

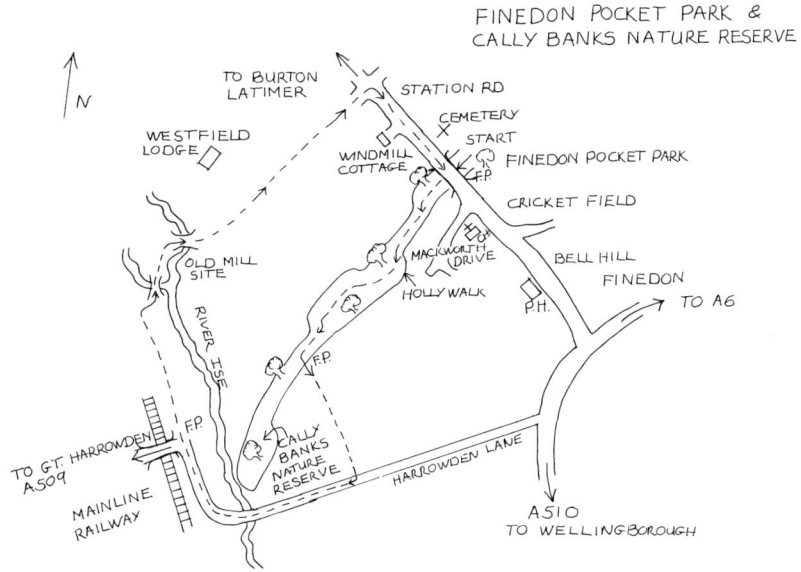

Recorded in Domesday Book as Tingdene, the town of Finedon straddles the A6 between Kettering and Bedford, where a glance over the roundabout at the A510 crossing reveals an eye-catching monument on a grassy mound.

The stone obelisk was erected by Sir English Dolben, lord of the manor, 'to record the many blessings of 1789', thought to refer to the recovery of George III from insanity at that time, but who was to relapse at a later date.

Sir English is remembered as a sensitive man who cared for his family and estate, though little but the name is left, yet the Hall retains its grandeur, set in spacious grounds amid magnificent trees.

The original ice-tower, then within the grounds of the Hall, where ice from the lake in winter was stored beneath, is now an integral part of a private house. Close by is Holly Walk, where the old limes are still interspersed with holly bushes, as in the past, though now wild and overgrown.

On the outskirts of the small town, Windmill Cottage, from 1818, was converted from a windmill into a residence by Mr Mackworth-Dolben, who also made alterations and additions to the Hall and The Bell Inn, to which he added a mock Gothic façade.

Claimed to be 'the oldest licensed house in England', built in 1598, it was to become a hostelry in 1830, replacing an earlier inn.

The striking water-tower on the main road, an abutressed structure of banded colour in the brickwork, built in 1904, is now a private residence. Originally intended to be accompanied by a swimming bath which was never to materialise.

WALK

Start at Station Road, near to the playing field, next to the cemetery at the top of the hill, where a pair of brick walls mark the dismantled railway line beneath. There is limited roadside parking for a couple of cars.

Finedon Pocket Park Stony Path

A fingerpost 'Finedon Pocket Park' indicates the path, which stretches in two directions, going forward to the park, to lead past the cricket field and back to the town.

The walk described here goes down the bank to double back along the old railway bed, initially passing under the road past a barrier put in place to deter hazardous motorbikes.

The temporary gloom is soon dispelled in this leafy tunnel and culminates as a bonus for birdwatchers. The track can be extremely wet and muddy, but cinder underfoot and remaining sleepers provide an alternative in some places. Flights of steps along the way give access to and from other directions, such as Holly Walk (for a shorter circuit), though not all are necessarily public footpaths.
Stay in the gully until the path gently rises up the embankment for about half a mile or more, as far as the three-fingered post directing to the Cally Banks Nature Reserve. To further enjoy the delights of this peaceful bower, continue on the raised bank, but be aware that there is no outlet at the farthest reaches.

The walk route now leaves the cover to descend to cross two fields to the Harrowden Lane. Turn right here and go over the River Ise, around the curve, now parallel with the main railway line. Very often there are cars parked on the bend, whose occupants are probably train-spotting!

Fingerpost at Finedon

Carry on forward through the metal gate, on the byway, ignoring the 'private' sign for the substation, heading for the far trees. Once over the little concrete bridge, the path turns sharply at a right angle to the river, opening up at a weir and pretty site of the former mill. Keep a watchful eye and wary approach, in the hope of spotting the elusive kingfisher. Take the winding way up the gentle slope, beside the ditch, looking back over the shoulder to the scoop of the compact shallow valley.

Over the field to the right, the unique Windmill Cottage is on the horizon.

Exit at the Burton Latimer road, opposite a neat industrial unit, to turn right to return to start on the safety of the pavement and the convenience of iron seats along the way.

FINEDON POCKET PARK AND CALLY BANKS NATURE RESERVE

Finedon Pocket Park, an important conservation area, occupies a strip of land two miles in length and in itself, a linear walk. The habitat is a result of an abandoned steep quarry face to an enclosed cutting, joining to the Cally Banks Nature Reserve at the far end.

Holly Walk – Finedon

Promoted by Northamptonshire County Council, it is open to the residents of the town, as well as visitors. Administered by the local branch of The Wildlife Trust, who are always on the look-out for volunteers to assist in the ongoing programme of work.

In the scrubland, native flowers are now established, such as the spotted and bee orchids, scabious, knapweed, rosebay willowherb and the shaggy teasel.

The ponds vary in capacity, according to weather conditions, but frogs, water-beetles and dragonflies are in abundance. In the more sheltered places, butterflies abound, including the meadow brown and skipper on their respective foodplants.

In the reserve, observe the woodpecker, goldfinch, redwing and the crafty cuckoo. Watch for the fleet of foot muntjac, tiny shrew and badger.

Cowslips

In spring, Holly Walk, a short remnant of spinney, leads from the cutting and bears catkins and wild cherry to brighten the way. In autumn, colour is added by hips and haws, sloes and blackberries, among the shiny berries of spindle. Beneath the trees, aconites, wood anemonies and snowdrops enhance the delights of this charming little offshoot.

PLACES OF INTEREST

HIGHAM FERRERS

The heart of Higham Ferrers lies in the vicinity of the Market Place, graced by the medieval Market Cross, from 1280, overlooked by the Town Hall built in 1809 at a cost of £755, having endured mixed fortunes as a market town.

Soaring above the immaculate limestone houses, the elegant carved steeple, 170 feet high, draws the eye to the parish church of St. Mary's, from the 13th century. In its shadow, the Chantry Chapel of 1422, has a chequered history and was used as a school until 1906.

Across the graveyard, the Bede House is in frequent demand and was refounded as a home for twelve elderly men and a female housekeeper. A penny a day pension and a fuel and clothing allowance was given in return for daily prayers and work, with strict rules for this regime, which ceased in the 18th century.

Marbled White Butterfly

Over the main street, Chichelle College accommodated a number of chaplains, clerks and choristers, whose devotions were enforced within the religious life of this building.

Henry Chichelle, a revered son of a local family, was born in 1362. Educated at Winchester under the patronage of the Lancaster family, he became close to Henry V and was appointed Archbishop of Canterbury in 1414, establishing the religious influence of the town and founder of the aforementioned bodies.

Other sites to visit might be Saffron Moat, commonly known as the 'cup and saucer', from the 15th century, which was used to provide fish for the ecclesiastical scholars and takes its name from the plant grown there to make medicine and dye.

The rough ground of the rabbit warren and fishponds is thought to be the site of an ancient motte and bailey from the time of the Conquest in 1066 and later a stone castle, whose material was 'recycled' for Kimbolton House in 1523, along with the Manor House, make a pleasant amble around Higham Ferrers an inviting proposition.

THE ROUND HOUSE

The Round House or Wellington Tower, on the A510 to the north of the town, yet within the parish of Burton Latimer, stands on a bend and is more difficult to observe in safety.

Constructed by the Reverend William Allington around 1815, when General Charles Arbuthnot of Woodfford House was host to the Duke of Wellington, who had remarked upon the likeness of the landscape to the terrain of the Battle of Waterloo.

The small turret was added, together with the bold inscription 'Panorama Waterloo Victory June 18 AD 1825' to this event. It was later to become a public house, then a club and currently is a private residence.

WALK 4

GLAPTHORN COW PASTURES AND SHORT WOOD NATURE RESERVES
Distance 2 miles
Map OS Landranger 151. 1:50 000
Grid ref: SP 006903
Nearest town – Oundle.

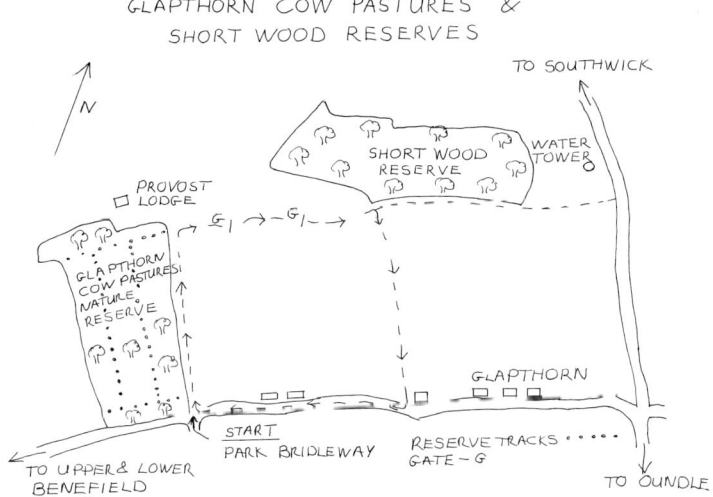

Little detail of the circuit is required here as it is fairly self evident. However, these reserves are of enormous interest to nature lovers and bird watchers, for their great potential.

As part of this, red kites may often be spotted in the skies in this area, as it was chosen as a release site, owing to the suitability of prey and other considerations.

A successful regeneration programme by English Nature for birds of prey which had become virtually extinct in this county, has proved highly productive and the birds are known to be thriving, despite some setbacks beyond the control of the instigators.

Buzzards too, have made a remarkable natural recovery, both of these species overwintering in the vicinity of Rockingham Forest.

WALK

Start at Glapthorn Cow Pastures, about one mile west of Glapthorn village, where parking is advised on the lower side of the marked bridleway.

A board at the entrance to the reserve shows the various paths and a roped trail for the blind, as well as the rides and glades, where the site is managed by The Wildlife Trust.

If desired, take a walk through the wood, where from time to time, guided walks are conducted to observe the black hairstreak butterfly, in early summer. The woodland is also a venue for the privilege of listening for the exquisite song of the much-loved nightingale.

Similarly, Short Wood has its own attraction and is deemed to be a superb setting for the glories of the bluebells and is likewise popular in early summer.

If the reserve is of no particular interest, or perhaps too wet and muddy, walk up the bridleway leading to Provost Lodge Farm. At the end of the wood, the footpath may be unmarked, but turn through the metal gate on the broad swathe of the ridge to follow 'Edward I's' perambulation of Rockingham Forest in 1299', a much-favoured hunting ground of the Plantagenet monarchy.

Blind trail Glapthorpe Cow Pastures

The path curves like a scythe to pass oak and ash trees affording vast dense tracts of forest to one side and a provocative glimpse of the needle spire of St. Peter's Church at Oundle, over the patchwork of fields.

Just prior to the corner of Short Wood, either take a wander around this second reserve or turn downhill on the stony track to exit close to the school at the village sign. Turn right to return along the fairly quiet road.

GLAPTHORN COW PASTURES NATURE RESERVE

The elusive black hairstreak butterfly is of great interest here in the latter end of June and the early days of July, but this may vary with the vagaries of warm weather conditions. The larvae feed on blackthorn bushes in the purposely managed glades and rides, where it is rewarding indeed to observe these unusual insects flitting high over the blossom.

Nightingales, sadly becoming less frequent in the countryside, breed in a part of the woodland and are best heard in the quiet and stillness of dusk in May and June.

Many other birds, such as the three types of woodpecker, treecreeper, nuthatch and tawny owl, inhabit this reserve.

The damp rides encourage abundant growth of meadowsweet, the early-purple orchid, bugle and dog's mercury, to list but a fraction of the flora of this 69 acre site, designated an SSSI (Site of Special Scientific Interest) and managed by The Wildlife Trust.

A specially laid out trail for the blind has been sensitively put in place, so that more may enjoy these peaceful bowers. Further details are available from The Wildlife Trust. Telephone 01604 405285.

SHORT WOOD NATURE RESERVE

This reserve is a 62 acre remnant of Rockingham Forest, wooded since medieval times and a close companion to the Cow Pastures. It uniquely comprises four woods within its perimeter: Cockshutt Close,

Dodhouse Wood, Hall Wood and Short Wood proper, each with its own history.

Perhaps it is best known, however, for the blooming carpet of fragrant bluebells in the dappled shades of early summer, when a series of guided walks, organised by The Wildlife Trust, take place on an annual basis and are locally advertised.

The reserve may also be independently accessed from the Glapthorn to Southwick road.

PLACES OF INTEREST

SOUTHWICK HALL

Three prominent families, the Knyvetts, Lynnes and the Caprons, owned the house successively from the early 14th century until the present day.

Two stair turrets and adjoining rooms of the original medieval house were built by Sir John Knyvett, who was Lord Chancellor to Edward III, and his forebears are still in evidence.
George Lynn, Sir John's descendant, who was a banner-bearer at the funeral of Mary Queen of Scots in 1587, rebuilt the south wing.

Further down the line, in the 18th century, another gentleman of the same name, added the west wing and made interior alterations, adding to the décor in Georgian style.

In the following century, an ancestor of the present owner, George Capron, extended the mansion, replenished the east wing and the stable block.

An exhibition of original Victorian garments is totally fascinating, in addition to a collection of external items in the courtyard, which give rise to a surge of reminiscence to visiting members of the public!

FOTHERINGHAY

Fotheringhay is a magnet for anyone with an interest in our past and continues to draw people from afar.

Little is left of the castle, just a meagre mound of earthworks, a pile of rough stones and in summer, tall Scottish thistles, referred to as 'Queen Mary's tears'. The queen was held captive from 1586 until her execution in the Great Hall on 8 February 1587 and there remains perhaps, a poignant ambience hanging over the river.

St Mary's and All Saints' College, was founded in 1411 by Edward, Duke of York, who was to die at Agincourt. The chancel was demolished by Dudley, Duke of Northumberland in 1573, which had been granted to him by Edward VI.

This lofty edifice, crowned by a landmark lantern tower, has a quiet and mysterious atmosphere, with grand Elizabethan memorials to Edward, second Duke of York, and Richard, third Duke of York, erected in 1573 by Elizabeth I.

Although the window panes are of clear glass in the church, do try to view the magnificent revival window of salvaged medieval glass shards in the tower, which is particularly effective on a sunny day, enhancing the curious symbols and colours.

A leisurely stroll through the village links two vital places in our chequered history.

WALK 5

GRETTON AND PADDOCK PARK
Distance 2 miles, steep in places
Map OS Landranger 152. 1:50 000
Grid ref: SP 899944
Nearest town – Corby

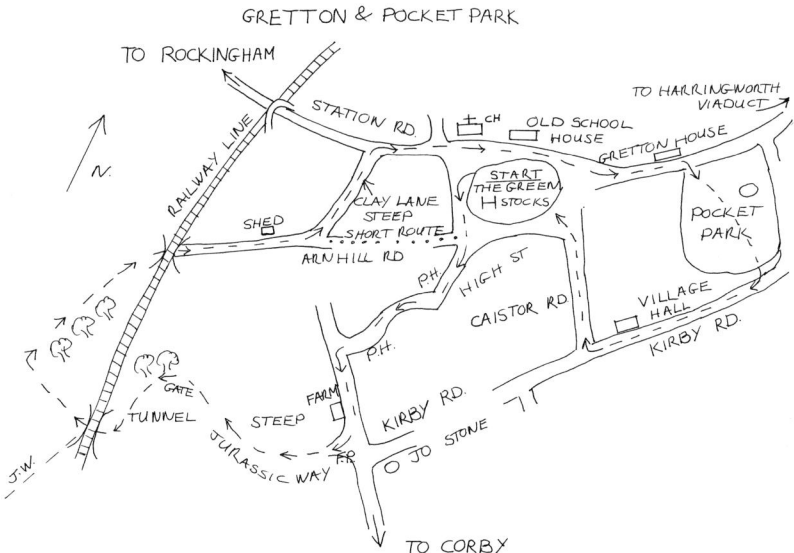

From The Green, facing the village store, walk along the High Street to the right, by the imposing Welland House and The Talbot public house, over School Road and the welcoming façade of The Bluebell Inn.

Round the bend, opposite the high stone wall at the junction with Kirby Road, stroll over to note the Jo stone, a boulder over which bargains and deals were struck and sealed by a handshake in days gone by.

Cross to Westhill Farm, now joining the long-distance footpath, the Jurassic Way, for a short spell, initially running between the buildings. At the gate an evocative prospect of the Welland Valley is revealed, where Rockingham Castle commands a strategic position on the distant hillside, though now partially obscured by trees, adding to its mystery. Several villages, Caldecott, Great Easton and Neville Holt lie scattered along the way over the river.

From this spot, a steep escarpment falls away in this one field and in summer, the railway line is almost hidden by the heavy growth on the embankment, where a kissing gate is close to the base before the tunnel. On emerging, the path immediately splits as the Jurassic Way diverges to the left, to Rockingham.

Stay on the shady track outside the field edge to keep a watchful eye and ear for a known family of green woodpecker and the possibility of spotting the soaring red kite.

Turn uphill through the next tunnel on the cinder surface of Arnhill Road, bordered by attractive detached homes.

The red brick hut is the original site of Gretton's Fire Station which housed an early horse-drawn, hand-pumped fire engine from 1858. Turning sharply to the lower level, Clay Lane, are the springs and ducts from which the water was drawn prior to the supply of mains water. If preferred and in order to dodge more hills, do not turn here but continue straight ahead to return to The Green.

Paddock Park – Gretton

Right at Station Road and uphill again, past 'Stoneycroft' (formerly known as The Sanctuary) with a unique stone inset beneath the eaves.

Either finish at the church or carry on past The Old Schoolhouse and cottage garden to the grand Georgian Gretton House. Opposite is the entrance to Paddock Park, for a quiet walk through to the far corner, then past the Village Hall, cutting Caistor Road to The Green.

PADDOCK PARK

Paddock Park, named by the village schoolchildren, is a pleasant grassland site of just over two acres, with the Jurassic Way running through it and probably a welcome respite for the weary walker.

The owners of Gretton House, facing, at one time held the land, when in use by the army in World War II, then taken over by British Steel, from whom the local Parish Council purchased the holding. It consequently became a Pocket Park, with assistance from Northamptonshire County Council, the 50th in the county, opened in 1995.

Gretton – Stocks on The Green

Tended by a hard working group of volunteers, it is a refuge not only in the cause of conservation, but for the peaceful pleasures of the local community.

An added bonus is the shelter and provision of habitat in the many mature trees, encircled by new plantings and the repair of the dry stone walls with unusual 'cock and hen' capping.

A bounteous butterfly bank has been created on a mound and planted to woo these insects, as dragonflies and damselflies take full advantage around the pond, an alluring aquatic habitat for a galaxy of other creatures too.

An original touch is the installation of a petanque court for the French game of boules, with useful seating for visitors.

Snowdrops in the spinney herald a year where events such as summer fetes, environmental plays and training days, have an ideal venue and children from the local school may have a safe and close-up access to observe nature in its many facets.

JURASSIC WAY

A recreational walking route of 88 miles, the Jurassic Way, passes through this county, linking to Banbury in Oxfordshire and beyond, to Stamford in Lincolnshire. It takes its name from the Jurassic Ridge, which rims the Welland Valley, weaving through the picturesque hamlets and villages, over a timeless landscape of open countryside. The distinctive logo on the waymark discs portray a fossil shell, Kallirhychia Sharpi, a brachiopod, named in honour of Samuel Sharp (1814-1882) an archaeologist and geologist, who lived at Dallington Hall, Northampton.

The fossils lie buried in the bedrock of the shallow seas which covered this land 165 million years ago.

Gretton Jo Stone

PLACES OF INTEREST

HARRINGWORTH VIADUCT

An important feat of engineering, officially known as the Welland Viaduct, in the Rockingham Forest area, utilised 20 million blue bricks of local clay and others of Derby flintstone, in the construction of the viaduct. From 1874 to its completion in July 1878, it was ultimately to carry the Kettering to Manston railway line.

Harrington Viaduct

Eighty-two arches averaging 57 feet in height, each with a 40 foot span and 3/4 of a mile long, it was the longest masonry viaduct in England. The provision of living accommodation for the huge workforce of hundeds of labourers, necessitated the building of forty huts at nearby Seaton End and twelve more at Gretton, plus space for about 120 working horses whose job it was to haul the waggons.

Among such an unwieldly disparate gang, accidents, hardships and fights were apparently legion and a Curate of the Railway Mission was often called upon to quell the frayed tempers of the motley!

KIRBY HALL

A grand Elizabethan mansion of Weldon stone, Kirby Hall is enhanced by the meticulously formal gardens in total keeping with the period. It is set entirely apart in this truly rural countryside, though modern commercial aspects do now occasionally impinge upon the silence.

Begun in 1570 by Sir Humphrey Stafford, who died in 1575, the estate was purchased by Sir Christopher Hatton, a favourite of Elizabeth I, whose principal residence at Holdenby House was not yet completed.

The first sight of this stunning façade and the strict symmetry of exquisite windows, present fine Renaissance detail.

The approach to the Hall is now to the rear, beside the decorative stone archway, making a much less dramatic impact than originally intended, as the effect through the short avenue of trees is now sadly diminished.

The courtyard gives access to the kitchen, buttery, pantry and domestic quarters and the labrynth of stairways and corridors invite exploration.

The Great Hall has a fine ceiling, where the timbers are carved with intricate foliage and the Great Staircase, in turn, led to the Long Gallery, which ran above the ground floor lodgings.

WALK 6

ISLIP AND TITCHMARSH LOCAL NATURE RESERVE
Distance 2 miles
Map OS Landranger 141. 1:50 000
Grid Ref: SP 986791
Nearest town – Thrapston

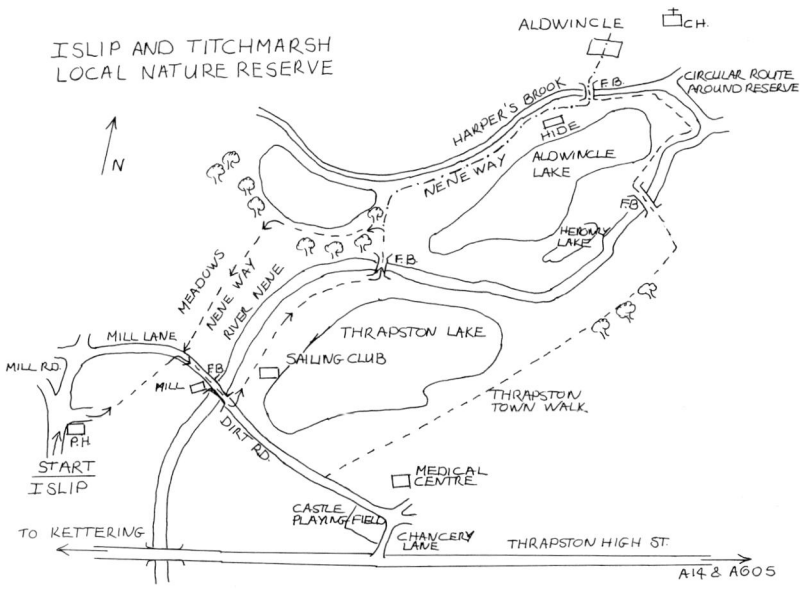

This might be described as a short genteel walk, but high in quality and an invitation to further exploration in the guise of Titchmarsh Local Nature Reserve, whose main approach is at the far end at Aldwincle, a village laced with history. There is also a Pocket Park, rejuvinating a previous eyesore to a welcome amenity.

Thomas Squire, who lived at Islip House next to the River Nene, was instrumental in opening up the Nene to navigation, which came to pass in 1737. He leased Islip Mill during this period, where corn was ground until 1960, but only the tastefully renovated house below the bridge serves as a reminder of the wharves and warehouses of this trade.

The premises of the current Working Men's Club were formerly the horse-collar factory, utilising rushes from the nearby river, for the stuffing of the collars and saddles.

Traces of the medieval packhorse/toll bridge may still be seen from the mooring bank, next to Thrapston Bridge, a handy spot to partake of a picnic on tables and benches just below road-level.

WALK

Park with discretion in the High Street in Islip, close to the Rose and Crown public house, as the Nene Way fingerpost points down through the car park, keeping to the left-hand side of the garden to the stile, to cross two fields diagonally.

On the way, admire the broad view over the River Nene and Thrapston town, making for a huge sycamore tree.

In Mill Lane for only a few yards, look over the fence to the mill pond adjacent to the tall Mill House, to go over the bridge and locks behind, to meet the dirt track, bearing left.

Mill-pond at Islip

The lake of the Mid-Nene Sailing Club is often busy with boats and wind-surfers to one side and the opposite bank of well colonised verges lead to patchy scrubland, alive with butterflies in summer and the soft purple hues of teasel.

Carry on for a while beside the water, watching for the set-back iron bridge leading into the nature reserve, but after crossing, turn sharply to the left. The Nene Way goes off in the opposite direction beside Harper's Brook toward Aldwincle and presents a further option to make a complete circuit of the reserve, which returns via Thrapston Town Walk, into the lane not far from the club.

Stay inside the spinney bordering the secluded lakes, to a double stile and planks over the ditch, to the flat water-meadows, as the steeple of Islip church rises above the confines of the village. At the barn, return as before or walk up Mill Lane back to the start point.

Bridge to Titchmarsh Nature Reserve

TITCHMARSH LOCAL NATURE RESERVE

This is a vast reserve of 179 acres, owned and managed by The Wildlife Trust since 1989, embracing a plethora of wildlife. First and foremost, the stretch of water comprises a number of islands and scrapes, where the levels are suited to waders, especially during the spring and autumn migrations.

Several of these islands, created after the extraction of gravel, accommodate thousands of birds, allowing them to nest undisturbed. An enormous colony of common terns is usually evident in summer.

A number of hides, including one dedicated to the naturalist Sir Peter Scott, who was an avid birdwatcher, gives both 'twitchers' and novices plenty of licence to enjoy the variety of species.

Winter is best and this is acknowledged as one of the top sites for the observation of wildfowl such as goosander, also Canada and Greylag geese. The dark cormorants present a somewhat macabre presence on overhead lines and isolated strips of land. Ringed and little plovers inhabit the shingle shores, where shelduck and oystercatchers also breed.

Watch out for the secretive darting kingfisher (known as 'halcyon' in early times) and overhead, the keen-eyed sparrowhawk, eternally seeking its prey.

The Heronry, created on the site of an old duck decoy by Lord Lilford, in the 19th century, is off-limits to visitors, owing to the sensitive breeding requirements of these haughty birds, but may be seen all year round from the banks and footpaths.

Large tracts of grassland are favourable to cowslips, sneezewort and great burnet and the more marshy land is colonised by speedwell, purple loosestrife and much more.

A wonderful display of butterflies include peacock, small tortoiseshell, common blue and small copper.

The flitting dragonflies live their short lives on the banks of the streams, the banded demoiselle agrion of subtle turquoise, the handsome common darter and the more aggressive hunting hawkers are among the masses.

The Nene Way, threads right through the reserve, from Islip to Aldwincle, but another marked path continues right around the lakes and on any of these, the best views are on the extended circuits.

PLACES OF INTEREST
LYVEDEN NEW BIELD

A few miles to the west, toward Corby on the A6116, just outside Brigstock, turn into Harley Way, signed Oundle, 3 miles east.

A National Trust property, this unfinished cruciform garden lodge in local limestone, was built between 1595 and 1605 by Sir Thomas Tresham of Rushton Hall.

Imprisoned for 13 years for his religious beliefs, he expressed himself in the moving testament of his faith, producing a major example of Elizabethan craftsmanship.

Surrounded by gardens, terraces and a moat where little sign lingers, it is planned to restore these features at some future date.

NENE WAY

The long-distance footpath, the Nene Way, follows the contours of the Nene Valley, from Badby, at the source of the river close-by at Arbury Hill, in the south of the county, meandering along to Wansford, on the county border, then carries on to The Wash. Very much an 'up hill and down dale' walk, it is a linking progression of footpaths and rights of way, taking the walker in short hops or the full distance, through both industrial and purely rural countryside.

In this instance, you may wish to extend your ramble beyond the nature reserve, to the delightful waterside village of Wadenhoe, via Aldwincle, a mile and a half each way.

On leaving the reserve, walk a short distance on the Aldwincle village loop road to Baulks Lane, a green cutting linking through to Main Street. Left past Pear Tree Farm to St. Peter's Church, where the Nene Way disc indicates the route.

Aldwincle has historical connections to famous figures of the past. One was John Dryden, born in 1631 at the rectory, now Dryden's Cottage and christened at All Saints', a striking church, now redundant, at the opposite end of the village, who was to become Poet Laureate to Charles II.

Another man of learning, Thomas Fuller, was born in the rectory of St. Peter's church in 1608, now replaced by a modern manse, who became curate of St. Benet's in Cambridge, a noted and revered historian and author of *'Worthies of England'*.

Initially along the ridge overlooking the winding river and its attendant water-meadows, the landscape cannot fail to delight the eye of the beholder. Going down beside Boathouse Spinney, do not miss the unusual stand of sequoias (redwoods) among the lesser trees, to go over the stream and fields, coming to a rough place named Conygher (rabbit warren). Emerge from the twisty path, with fresh picturesque cameos around every bend, below the ancient church of St. Michael and All Angels, with its saddleback roof, uncommon in this county, standing alone on the crest of the hill.

Inside these solid walls are memorial plaques to the local prominent family, the Ward-Hunts, residents of Wadenhoe House, one of these recording a particularly poignant tale of a young married couple and others of important persons.

On the gentle path, accompanied by the soothing sounds of the water, the outstanding Millennium sundial in perfect proportions of slate and stone, gives valuable information.

In the months of summer, linger awhile at the Village Hall for a delicious cream tea or enjoy the riverside gardens of the adjacent public house, in this county gem, a favoured spot for visitors.

Walk 3. Old railway track – Finedon

Walk 2. Near Purston – Sweeping pastures

Walk 4. Black hairstreak butterfly – Glapthorn Cow Pastures

Walk 5. Wakerley Woods

COLOUR PLATE III

Walk 7. Brightwells Lake – Little Addington

COLOUR PLATE IV

Walk 10. Stoke Wood environs

COLOUR PLATE V

Walk 11. Clouded yellow butterfly – Summer Leys Reserve

Walk 11. Summer Leys Nature Reserve – secluded pond

Blaze of poppies

COLOUR PLATE VII

Walk 12. Twywell Hills & Dales Gullet

COLOUR PLATE VIII

WALK 7

KINEWELL LAKE NATURE RESERVE AND ENVIRONS
Distance approximately 6 miles
Map OS Landranger 141. 1:50 000
Grid ref: SP 980750
Nearest town – Thrapston

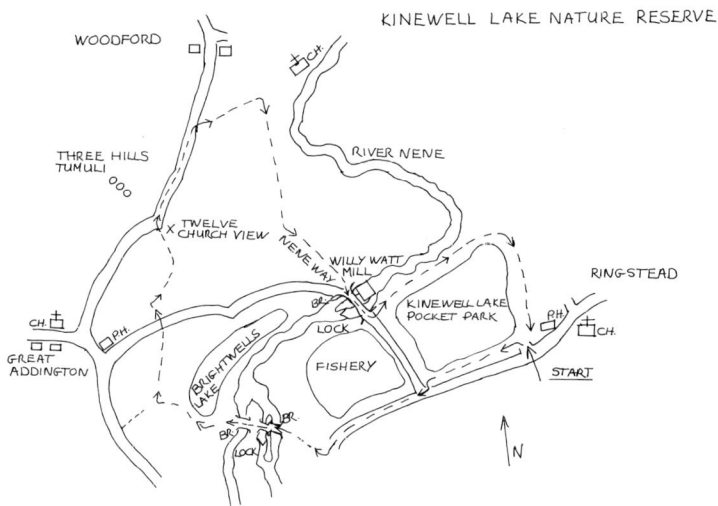

There are various loops to shorten this ramble, though the one described enables the walker to enjoy infinite stretches of land and water.

River valleys were always the obvious places for settlements back through the ages and this section is no exception.

Further along, below Stanwick, a prolific archaeological dig a few years ago, found valuable evidence of a Roman settlement, with not only streets, houses, bathhouses and a huge circular well, but most importantly, two spectacular mosaic floors buried only just below the surface of the field and barely disturbed by consequent farming. The original colours of the small tesserae were still discernable. Unfortunately, there was only limited time for this project, which was then exposed to further gravel extraction, later flooded and lost for ever.

Other exploration has uncovered treasure, such as at Irchester, where a cache of Roman coins was found, also finds at Stanwick and Raunds nearby.

The medieval deserted village of Mallows Cotton is just off the track. The direct cause for its abandonment is not known for sure, but one quote (in more than 80 such cases in Northamptonshire) from 1356, referring to another disaster, is that no-one dwells there 'since the pestilence and the land is wasted by the king's deer'.

WALK

Start at the Kinewell Lake Nature Reserve on the outskirts of the village of Ringstead to walk, with the lake to the right, parallel with the road on the outer side of the hedge, to exit at the T-junction, opposite the trout fishery.

Cross directly to the lane of the old bed of the uplifted rail line, past Ringstead Grange Fishery, where the track becomes less salubrious (but will soon change!) before bearing right at the former site of the old railway station and Mallows Cotton medieval deserted village.

Kinewell Lake Nature Reserve at dusk

Go over the bridge and lock, to note the neglected and almost overgrown string of massive stones, a forgotten relic used by foot passengers over the swampy ground, from the nearby communities to the station.

Brightwells Lake restores tranquility and displays a diagram showing the extent of the Countryside Stewardship Scheme, allowing open access.

Stay on a straight forward line, to go through the hedgerow gap just prior to a path joining from the left, on the first field headland, shifting to the second field and stile, with Great Addington in sight. For village and pub turn left uphill at the road or right back to the reserve.

Otherwise, cross the road (no sign) under a trio of telegraph poles next to a spinney, as it curves briefly upward, watching for two adjacent stiles on the left and up again toward the uncluttered skyline. A remnant of a stile doubles as a seat, as the way ahead tips over the top into the unseen and unknown at this point!

Abandoned Stepping-stones to old Ringstead Station

A disc now indicates the direction of the water-tower, beleaguered under a mass of aerials, as the Nene Valley unfolds in a kaleidoscope of subtle colour, from this route of an old Roman road.

Exit here on a lazy S-bend to a gateway with a wide verge, where the humps of Three Hills Tumuli over the road, on the horizon, may be reached by public footpath if desired.

On a fine day, the canvas of the River Nene and water meadows provide a sweeping panorama to include twelve churches, ten with spires and two with towers: Woodford, Thrapston, Denford, Islip, Ringstead, Stanwick, Raunds, Irthlingborough, Rushden and Little Addington, have the former and Great Addington and Titchmarsh, the latter.

Walk beside the road for a few moments and just past the turning to the marina, the footpath sign and little plank bridge may be hidden by growth in summer, leads downhill. A tantalising spread beckons, particularly toward Woodford, where the the spire of St. Mary's church bursts from the trees, via the Nene Way, left and another site of a medieval settlement. However, down the slope and turn right to double back at the gate to resume the circuit, not far from the river, as the route is determined on a low line, crossing the concrete marina access to continue through scrub over the water-meadows. Allow for possible flooding in winter.

Brightswell Lake through the rushes

Follow the the footpath signs, rising a little before reaching Willy Watt Mill. Hover by the setting of the river and locks, as this is a busy place in the summer season, for boats and fishermen. Turn through the natty 'squeeze stile' into the nature reserve, either way on an established path around the lake to savour the peace of this tranquil park, to return to start.

KINEWELL LAKE NATURE RESERVE
(KINEWELL TRUST)

A prime example of 87 acres of biological diversity, with five freshwater lakes encapsulated by reedbeds, marshland and patches of woodland planted in the last century.

These areas provide superb habitats for myriad insects, where butterflies and dazzling dragonflies hunt and hover over the waters.

Of special note, is the rare insect, the Longhorn Beetle, now found in very few places.

Perhaps the most popular bird would be the great crested grebe, or the elusive kingfisher, seeking small fish and aquatic prey. The stately herons are elegant eye-catchers and in winter the lake plays host to hundreds of ducks, such as the shoveller, who alight here to partake of the nutritious waters.

Owls, hawks and mammals thrive in this reserve whose pollarded willows grace the banks and selective thinning of woodland encourages growth, not only of the trees, but also enhances the ground beneath.

This method, though labour intensive, allows a longer life for the trees, which in turn houses plants, insects and frequently mosses and lichens. The resulting holes become magnets for nest-sites for many species of birds and bats, the latter having lost a range of lofts and countryside barns. The typical contorted root systems are a haven for more shy creatures and consequently, the tree takes on an essential role as a micro hideaway in itself for both residents and transients!

PLACES OF INTEREST

NATIONAL DRAGONFLY BIOMUSEUM

Although about 10 miles to the north, the museum has the only authentic dragonfly reserve in Europe.

Based in a former 18th century estate mill, in itself a singular building, this unique museum highlights the wonder of these exquisite insects, bringing them into close range with unusual exhibits.

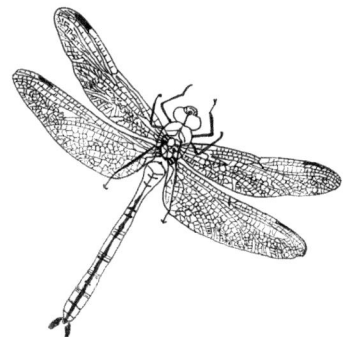

The dashing dazzlers are one of the species of insects which are slowly diminishing. So little is known about them, although 39 species are recognised in Britain, this learning facility brings to the fore the importance of research and a more intimate knowledge to the observer, via a microscopic videolink and essential information.

Wetlands are vanishing at an alarming rate and habitats declining for various environmental reasons. Every care must be taken to protect these colourful dragonflies and damselflies, who do us a service by devouring gnats, midges and mosquitoes – some of the more troublesome of the family.

> *I gazed at the dragonfly with sheen on sheer wings–*
> *How does it fly on such gossamer strings?*
> *How does it hover, sighting its prey?*
> *Then off it soars to hunt far away.*
> *Eyes bulging green with ferocious glare,*
> *Mouth all a-quiver it darts through the air,*
> *But now lies quite dead, attacked by a foe,*
> *Though wings feebly flutter when gentle winds blow.......*
>
> *Mia*

Broad-bodied chaser dragonfly

River Nene

WALK 8

PITSFORD WATER AND NATURE RESERVE
Distance 3 miles
Map Landranger 141. 1:50 000
Grid ref: OS 780703
Nearest town – Northampton

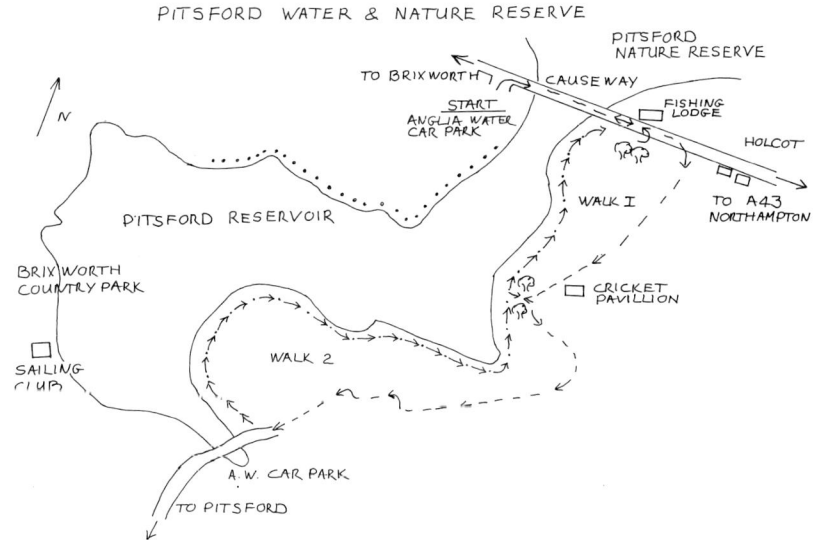

Two, or maybe even three walks, for the price of one, must be a provocative invitation, such as offered here!

Pitsford Water is a worthy choice of venue for the walker and cyclist who appreciate the lure of both water and wildlife – especially for those handy with the camera.

A sinuous track of 8 miles clings to the shoreline, with a visual treat around every curve.

Lying on the opposite side from the walks circuit, Brixworth Country Park is attainable via the dam on foot, where the nature reserve over the Causeway only adds to the perks of this stunning location.

WALK 1

Begin at the Anglian Water car park at the northern end of the Causeway, with wide stretches of water on either side. Continue up the hill toward the village of Holcot, ignoring the spinney entrance on the right, which becomes the exit on the return route.

Just prior to the first house, go through the split fence to start on a downward slope, as extensive views are soon to be revealed. The path descends quickly and fairly steeply, beside a plantation, to a bridge, where water tumbles down the bank from an unseen source.

Bear slightly to the right through a wide gap, as the grass track goes up and over the rise, next to a cricket pavilion topped by a cupola and clock, over the hedge. Cross the avenue of young lime trees to the broad green swathe and just prior to the horse jumps, turn away at the fingerpost in the hedgerow, to change direction at right angles and again at the facing headland, down to a conglomeration of kissing-gates at the parting of the ways.

The path now divides, going on to Pitsford (2 miles) but for the lesser circuit, go through the trees toward the water, to bear right on to the access track to head back to the distant Causeway, to eventually exit through light woodland and return.

Pitsford Water – Clutch of gates!

WALK 2

To extend this pleasant and rewarding walk as far as Pitsford, from the gates aforementioned, carry on up the hill, keeping to a similar line to follow the discs up hill and down dale.

A scattering of more isolated dwellings dot the route, which finally runs downhill between wooden rail fencing to Pitsford.

Just before the lodge, a path loops around the water's edge to rejoin the first section or goes on ahead into Pitsford village.

PITSFORD WATER NATURE RESERVE

By comparison to others, this is indeed, a massive reserve and the visitor may only catch but a glimpse of the wildlife hidden away in its far reaches. It is necessary to obtain a permit to peruse this area, which includes the complete perimeter walk of 7 miles.

Pitsford Water was constructed to provide water for the county town and began to operate in 1955. Later, The Wildlife Trust took on the management of the site and in 1970, the 486 acres was given SSSI (Site of Special Scientific Interest) status.

Pitsford Water panorama

Streams filtering into the lake form 'arms' and shallow water creates shelter and sustenance for winter wildfowl. As the seasons progress, the subsequent muddy patches provide nourishment for migrating waders, where such havens are a protection against disturbance.

It is estimated that up to 10,000 assorted ducks find refuge here including 24 of the species, as well as 3 species of divers and 5 of grebes. Mute swans, Canada geese, whooper swans and periodically Bewicks swans, winter flocks of fieldfare, redwing and blackbirds on berries, foraging tits and goldcrest.

A rookery of 200 nests houses the usual collection of birds, where the raucous multitudes evidently find breeding conditions conducive to their needs.

Unusual plants flourish on the exposed mud and water-loving greenery colonises the fringes. Many host plants accommodate galls.

Butterflies, dragonflies and damselflies are legion and the wetland is home to amphibians and reptiles, particularly grass snakes, prevalent in summer, where basking spots are ideal for the purpose. Also 100 plus species of spider have been recorded, among a host of mammals.

Pitsford Water Nature Reserve

It would take a lifetime of visits to observe the infinite and agreeable biodiversity of flora, fauna and all that is contained therein!

Permits are required to enter the reserve, from The Lodge, which are free to members of The Wildlife Trust, for others there is a small charge.

PLACES OF INTEREST

BRIXWORTH COUNTRY PARK

The development of Brixworth Country Park by Northamptonshire County Council, since its inception in 1990, has resulted in a popular amenity, not only for all age groups, but especially for the blind and is also wheelchair friendly. These groups and individuals are encouraged by conveniently laid out access paths and a sensory garden.

The outlook over Pitsford Water and the Sailing Club is quite stunning and within the David MacIntosh Centre, are the Ranger's Office, shop and information desk, cafeteria and other facilities. There is bicycle hire and overnight accommodation for organised groups on environmental courses.

The open land is excellent for kite-flying adjacent to a boules court and picnic area. There is a guided walks programme, in addition to access to the Brampton Valley Way, a linear walk between Northampton and Market Harborough along the defunct railway line on a designated track.

Umbellifer

NORTHAMPTON AND LAMPORT RAILWAY TRUST

A comprehensive display of rolling stock including steam and classic diesel locomotives with some in the process of restoration. It is run by members of the Preservation Society, with a regular passenger timetable, for fun weekends and a host of special events. The Brampton Valley Way runs alongside most of the railway track bed.

LAMPORT HALL

Home of the Isham family from 1560 to 1976, with a 17th and 18th centuries façade by John Webb and the Smiths of Warwick.

A wealth of fine paintings, furniture and china are only a fraction of the treasures contained here. The gardens were laid out in 1655 and later, in the 19th century, by Sir Charles Isham, 10th Baronet, who created the Italian Garden Rockery, introducing the first garden gnomes into this country.

Museum, giftshop and tearooms, a summer season of arts and some entertainments are based in the Elizabethan stables.

Enigmatic grey heron

WALK 9

STOKE BRUERNE AND NATURE RESERVE
Distance about 1 mile
Map OS Landranger 152. 1:50 000
Grid ref: SP 745500
Nearest town – Northampton

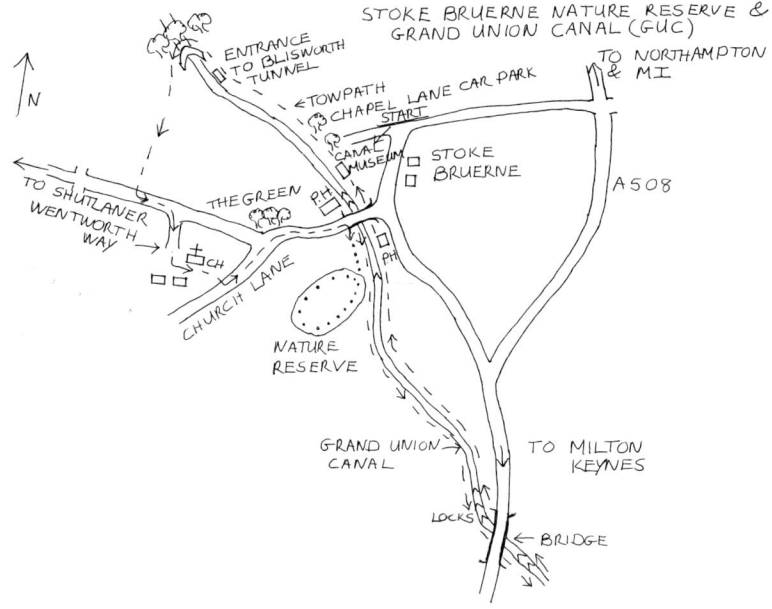

Folk 'messing about in boats' has always been true of the English and being so far from the coast, our canals and rivers are forever busy. Boat owners and those less fortunate are drawn to such places as Stoke Bruerne on the Grand Union Canal and even in winter, there is usually some movement there.

A bridge now means that risking life and limb mincing over the top of the lock gates or crossing by the old hump-backed bridge, is lost to us, in the cause of safety!

A visit to the museum, or the nature reserve, pubs, restaurants and teashops, allow plenty of choice, but the focus is, of course, on the bright narrow-boats with polished brasses and the traditional hand-painted utensils. The care lavished on these craft is a testament to the persuance of the lifestyle of those who divorce themselves from speed and thankfully, noise.

It is a great place for exploration, with the old towpaths, where horses plodded along yoked with the burden of heavy loads, with the promise of a loaded nosebag, the flight of locks, where the pace cannot be hurried and echoes of the past ways of life, still exist.

WALK

Start at the Canal Museum on the towpath, where there are a number of interesting original signs and equipment relevant to the waterways, next to the official car park. Turn right beside the trees and picnic tables for this neat little circuit.

Just beyond the 'winding pool' a turning point for narrow boats, is a small stable, where horses who had laboured to pull the boats, could stand in the shade, and were fed and watered awaiting the next job.

Blisworth Tunnel yawns ahead in the darkness, so take the path up the embankment but before the incline straightens out, a distinctive disc shows the way over the top, through the trees to open to a diagonal path over the fields.

At the road to Shutlanger, bear left to soon cross at Wentworth Way, a dead end. In front of the far house, the path leads to the church. Pause to puzzle at the inscription on the gate pillar, then zig-zag through the graveyard into Church Lane, opposite the Village Hall, to rejoin the road edging The Green.
Before the bridge, opposite The Boat Inn, a recessed metal gate has a sign for The Wildlife Trust Reserve, on the site of the old brickworks.

To further extend this walk by about a mile with a grand opportunity to take a closer look at this fascinating piece of history, take the towpath on the lower side to follow the flight of seven descending locks as far as the A508 or beyond, to cross the canal wherever convenient, to return on the other side, next to the hostelry.

If not crossing the water, retrace your steps to go under the road bridge, up the steps, for a look at the original dry dock and explanatory plaque before returning to the museum and car park.

Stoke Bruerne – Canal Museum

STOKE BRUERNE NATURE RESERVE

An earlier site of the brickworks, producing material for the Grand Union Canal, but becoming unviable about 1920, with a brief revival after the Second World War. The bricks were utilised in the construction of nearby Blisworth Tunnel, as well as for locks, walls and sideponds, where there are a few visible remains.

The low-lying wetland, leased to The Wildlife Trust in 1988, has ponds, copious reedbeds, marshes and patchy scrub, encompassed by an easy path for access.

Flowers such as adder's tongue fern, common spotted orchid and sweet-smelling meadowsweet are surrounded by hawthorn, field maple and dogrose. In the damp places, ragged robin, bird's-foot trefoil and the cuckoo flower prevail and reed warblers and yellowhammers find convenient perches. Ponds and reedbed habitats encourage snipe, moorhen, coot and reed-bunting, unconcerned by the stately sharp-eyed heron who dips there too. Barn owls and kestrel find this an ideal hunting ground, abundant with small mammals.

Grass snakes and insects do well in this environment, which is adjacent to the towpath, separated by a low wall, just below the bridge.

PLACES OF INTEREST
CANAL MUSEUM AND BLISWORTH TUNNEL

The Canal Museum, part of the Waterways Trust, is right alongside the Grand Union Canal and portrays 200 years of waterways history.

Originally a corn mill, this splendid three storey stone conversion now houses an unmatched collection of the daily lives of canal folk and their colourful, sturdy boats.

The trade and traditions are faithfully displayed, including equipment, both inside and about the exterior of the place. Hand-painted examples of Canalware on a variety of everyday utensils, often incorporating a castle, plus other unique artefacts, add atmosphere.

The history and background of the waterways, from the inception as a trading route in 1793, to present day use, is graphically illustrated, as well as the precise details of the innovative, for its time, Blisworth Tunnel.

This tunnel is the longest navigable tunnel in Britain, at 1 3/4 miles in length. Opened in 1805, linking two sections of canal, boats were urged through the damp darkness by 'leggers'. Previously, horses hauling from the towpath had to be unharnessed and led over the hill, together with any cargo, over a makeshift railway, then put into ropes again to continue the journey.

When the new tunnel was finally completed and opened for business, the 'leggers' laid on their backs on boards slung across the decks of the boats and 'walked' the dank roof.

Grand Union Canal

At the introduction of a tug service in 1861, the primitive horse-drawn railway became obsolete and after further years of modification, boats proceeded through under their own steam.

An amusing term applied to people hanging over the bridge or dallying by the locks was a 'gongoozler'!

Museum shop, boat trips and canalside walks, teas etc., in summer. Allied courses, family events and educational visits may be arranged.

TOWCESTER RACECOURSE

The Racecourse is a part of the spacious parkland estate and family residence of Lord Hesketh at Easton Neston, where the imposing gateway fashioned in 1822, was the approach to the manor.

There are three enclosures, Jump and Arab horse meetings, and a comprehensive fixture list. Other events, such as classic and pop concerts, spectaculars, vintage motorcycles etc., are as advertised.

WALK 10

STOKE WOOD END QUARTER AND ENVIRONS
Distance 3 miles
Map OS Landranger 141. 1:50 000
Grid ref: SP 790867
Nearest town – Desborough

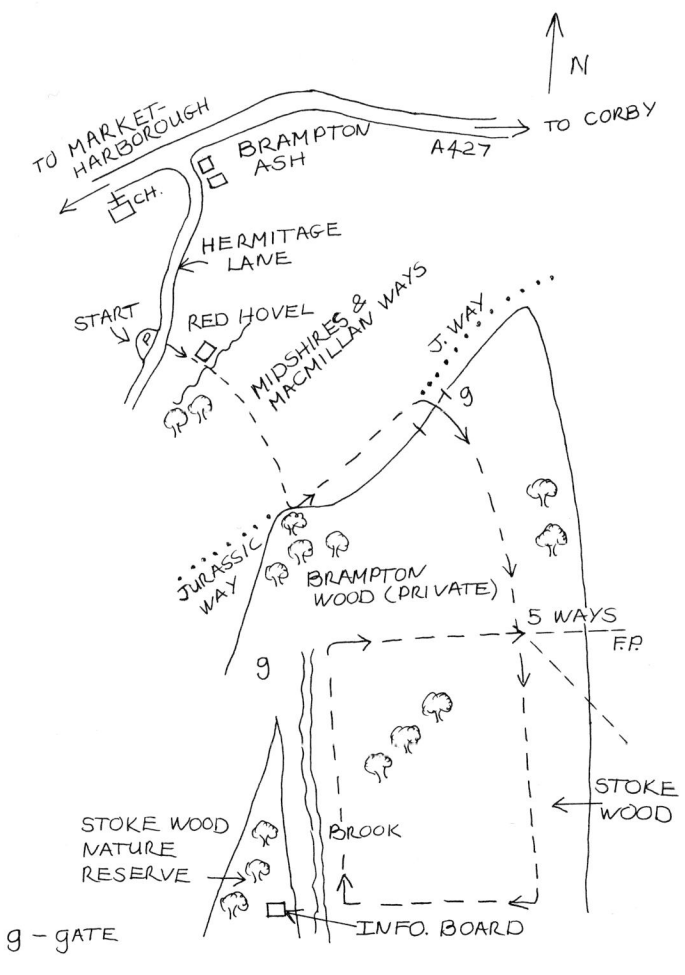

The River Welland is the county boundary between Northamptonshire on the south side and Leicestershire.

The rift was formed as a result of the Jurassic Ridge, a limestone escarpment, hence the drop to the floor of the Welland Valley, causing the undulating terrain of the slopes.

The Macmillan Way is another long-distance walking route, only a short section of which runs on the same line as the Jurassic Way.

It is a waymarked coast-to-coast path from Boston in Lincolnshire to Abbotsbury in Dorset, of 290 miles, roughly following the ridge. Opened in 1996 it wends its way south through ten counties.

It therefore follows that the landscape here, back from the edge of the acutal valley, is one of great beauty and as far as the eye can see, fold upon gentle fold of green pastures and wedges of woodland, are undeniably beautiful.

WALK

From the A27 Corby to Market Harborough road, turn off south at the village of Brampton Ash into Hermitage Lane, close to the church.

East Carlton Park ver Welland Valley

As the surface flattens out at the base of the hill, there is a meagre patch suitable for parking, opposite a metal gate and fingerpost.

Across the field Red Hovel (as marked on OS map) is a group of red-brick sties and a stockyard, ahead of the gatepost with logos of the Macmillan and Midshires Ways.

On the hill, a neat path follows the hedgeline toward the dense growth of Brampton Wood. After a short, steep pull, catch a moment at the summit to turn back to look over the pastoral folds to the Welland Valley, in the distance.

On arrival at the corner of the wood, leaving the Midshires Way, do not attempt to enter the trees but swing left to continue on the broad swathe of the perimeter, now briefly on the Jurassic Way, as every curve exposes a changing panorama.

On the final downward wooded edge before the visible end of the thicket, seek the sunken gate in the wire fence, which may easily be overlooked when one is occupied with such tantalising vistas.

Stoke Wood – Jurassic Way logo

Down the bank and over the ditch, muddy patches may occur at almost any time of the year, as both high tree canopy and heavy ground cover can be dense, keeping out sunlight in places, but producing enchanting dappled paths and glades in summer.

The path goes straight ahead uphill, narrowing here and there, sliding between occasional palings. As it rises, the protracted tunnel effect is enhanced by way-off glimpses of the sky at the far end. In quiet sheltered spots under the trees, low plaques bear the names of past devotees of this countryside.

At the less obvious meeting ways, five footpaths converge, keep forward to the next crossing to turn right into a slit of a woodland track, going down into the dell.

A noticeboard gives details of the sliver of The Wildlife Trust property, Stoke Wood End Quarter, a tiny wedge between the Brampton Wood and The Woodland Trust segment, Stoke Wood.

On leaving the reserve, keep to the path in the dip, with a ditch to the left, as far as the gate high on the bank, then start climbing upward to the right, which meets the main path at the five ways intersection. Turn left back down to exit into daylight to reverse the outward route.

STOKE WOOD END NATURE RESERVE

Resembling the pointy leaf of the cuckoo pint when viewed on the map, this reserve is a wee gem! It may be small, but tread warily, for it is packed with goodies to fill the eye and the senses.

DORMOUSE PROJECT

The core of the patch and indeed along with its Woodland Trust neighbour, comprising Stoke Wood, is managed jointly, in specific support of the dormouse. This tiny defenceless mammal, whose entire existence is threatened, clings to a tenuous lifeline in our countryside of diminishing resources, making this a haven of extreme importance.

Search among the leaf litter to examine the discarded hazel nuts to note the differences between the dormouse and bank vole, who each leave a distinctive clue in the pattern of teethmarks in the hard shells.

The coppiced woodland allows the hazel trees to flourish and admits stimulating light to encourage the growth of bramble, a food source for these diminutive animals and honeysuckle for the weaving of their nests. A quote from Rossetti on the honeysuckle flower is "virgin lamps of scent and dew".

These elusive creatures of shiny eyes and golden fur, live above ground level where there is ample cover, seldom venturing down to the woodland floor. They utilise the intricate aerial runways to scamper back and forth, before retiring to their summer nests in especially rigged nestboxes, out of reach of their prospective predators.

Fallow and muntjac deer do well here, in seclusion, where agile treecreepers and nuthatch scavenge the treetrunks in their constant hunt for insects. Overhead, sparrowhawks drop from the sky to swoop on prey at the woodland edge and woodpeckers are not uncommon.

Tall oaks, ash and field maple are common and ground cover is thick with the mass of flora and vegetation.

Stoke Wood was designated an SSSI (Site of Special Scientific Interest) in 1954.

Stoke Wood End Quarter Doormouse Project

PLACES OF INTEREST
EAST CARLTON COUNTRYSIDE PARK

East Carlton Countryside Park of 100 acres, to the east of Corby, owned and managed by Corby District Council, has something to draw all ages, each with diverse interests.

Not least, is the perfect setting graced by the elegant Hall, a private residence overlooking the verdant Welland Valley.

Outside the lower perimeter fence, is the long-distance footpath, the Jurassic Way, in this vicinity, linking Wilbarston to Middleton.

Apart from the wide open spaces with mature trees and a fixed trail, the former stable block of the mansion has been transformed to become a craft centre and museum. The latter features the past industrial heritage of the area, opencast mining for ironstone, which was then conveyed by trucks on rails to the famous steelworks of Stewart and Lloyds at Corby. Models of the massive draglines are on display and outside on the paved forecourt, ingots and chains represent this industry.

A cafeteria, playground and much more in the way of events combine to cater for the needs and pleasures of the visitors.

ROCKINGHAM CASTLE

'900 years of living history' is no idle boast, for William the Conqueror built the castle on a prime hilltop site of an earlier ancient British fortress, with later construction by Edward I in the 13th century. Commanding a dominant presence, the mighty, imposing gateway of Weldon stone, sets the scene.

Medieval kings went out from these stout walls to hunt in the sweeps of Rockingham Forest and the Tudor Henry VIII granted a lease to Edward Watson in 1553, who converted the fortress into a family house.

Witness to the English Civil War, as a Royalist stronghold, it was attacked by Oliver Cromwell's Roundheads and the ensuing siege is one of the enactments currently portrayed between the Cavalry and the Roundheads.

The castle is a veritable treasure-chest, as is the Great Hall, the main Staircase, the Library and the Long Gallery, most of which may be seen on a guided tour.

In the Victorian era, Charles Dickens drew inspiration for his writings here and was purported to have witnessed a lady ghost drifting between the ancient topiary of the 'elephant' yew hedge which never fails to attract the attention of visitors to the 12 acres of spacious gardens.

There are intriguing paths to explore the dells and reaches of parkland, well studded with long-standing trees, all these combine to provide a magical ambience.

The church, on a lower level, dedicated to St. Leonard, has a memorial chapel to honour the ancestors of the present owners, the Watsons.

It was the site chosen for the BBC TV series 'By the Sword Divided' serialising a family caught up in the English Civil War conflict.

A gift shop, tea room, guided tours and a plethora of special events are offered throughout the year.

WEST LODGE RURAL CENTRE

A farm park to captivate anyone who loves animals, with some to pet, tractor rides, woodland walks and farm trails and special programmes for children.

WALK 11

SUMMER LEYS LOCAL NATURE RESERVE AND GREAT DODDINGTON

Distance: Reserve walk 2 miles – including Great Doddington 3 miles
Map OS Landranger 152. 1:50 000
Grid ref: OS 885633

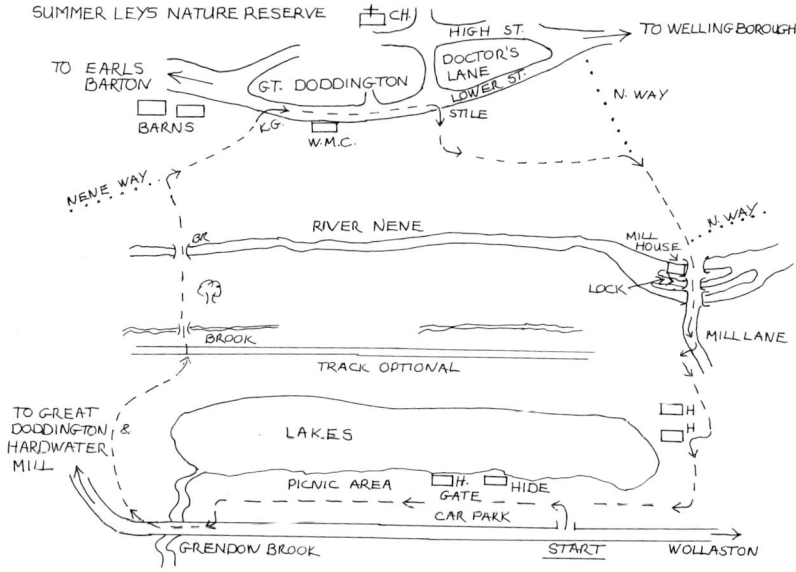

Summer Leys has quickly gained a reputation as a wetland mecca for birdwatchers, nature lovers and walkers, drawing people from beyond the county borders.

Several birdhides, one large enough to accommodate a whole class of schoolchildren, another specifically designed for the wheelchair user, enabling the occupant to sit right up close to the open window.

In the far corner, a hide dedicated to a local man, opens to an immediate and more intimate patch where birds of many persuasions gather at this feeding station. Devouring fallen apples, grain and seed, thus allowing the observer a close-up of individual species, as well as a snapshot view over the more distant lakes.

The leys, a reminder of the original meadows, has been developed under the auspices of Northamptonshire County Council and English Nature and managed by the Nene Valley Project. However, the hard graft invested in the early preparation when many journeys were undertaken to bring in water-loving plants from another site about to be invaded by diggers, has paid off. The current day-to-day jobs are conscientiously carried out by a dedicated team of volunteers whose skills are legion and must be applauded.

The circular walk reveals all sorts of nooks and crannies, so be prepared for a surprise at any time of the year.

WALK

There is plenty of space for parking at the reserve, so, facing the picnic meadows, leave through the gate to the left, over the little bridge, to initially follow the circuit signs. Several seats en route look over the waters from a number of places to view the changes from summer to winter, both of flora and wildlife, especially of the migrating birds who call here.

The path is briefly diverted where Grendon Brook flows under the road in a stone-banked culvert and very often, fish may be spotted here on lazy days, though fast flows the water when floods are threatening.

Summer Leys Nature Reserve Nene Valley

Once past the bridge, the flat course edged by young trees, stretches ahead to the old disused track, which used to have a lengthy conveyor belt carrying quarried gravel, when commercial extraction occupied this area. Now the stony track and tall hedges form excellent cover for wildlife and give aspects of the islands and hides.

To take the circular walk of the reserve only, bear right to follow the discs. Otherwise, for the complete circuit, cross the track and wooden bridge, making for Great Doddington on the ridge, over the water-meadows to a lone tree, then an iron-sided hump-backed bridge over the river, making sure to secure the gate.

Straight on to join the Nene Way at the rail fence and stile, traversing two hilly fields, keeping well away from a green shed, shortly into a dip and up again, with bigger green barns and yard to the left, to the farthest corner to exit at the tall white gate and right into Lower Street. Walking along, take note of the delectable dwellings, with provocative glimpses of well-tended gardens inside mellowed stone walls, enhanced in between by snatches of superb valley vistas.

Very soon, opposite Doctor's Lane (straight up and over the main street to visit the ancient church of St. Nicholas in Church Lane), a fingerpost and quaint 'slab' stile in the stone wall, defines the way, as the path slips down a narrow passage between fence and hedge, to regain the pastures via a kissing-gate.

The rather gloomy path soon bursts from confinement to a steep slope in a contained 'scoop' through the next couple of kissing-gates, to bear left over the hill and a fourth gate, leading diagonally to rejoin the Nene Way at a stile on the crest, just prior to a white metal gate. The limestone ridge now enables the walker to survey and appreciate the watery spread of the reserve and the Nene Valley. Wollaston lies directly beyond on the far side and on a clear day, St. Mary's church at Whiston is visible on Combe Hill.

The fields fall away toward the river, where the Nene Way departs along the bank to Wellingborough. Instead, through the gate beside the pond, the gravel path passes in front of the isolated private residence on the site of the old mill. By the huge gates and the thunder of water at Wollaston Lock, leisure boats are often moored on the banks of this secluded backwater.

Over the bridge, turn right for a short way, then left down the slope and gate to re-enter the reserve, skirting ponds and lakes. The feeding station makes a perfect place to halt for a breather and watch the birds enticed by a common cause – food!

Carry on around the perimeter and further hides, to return to base.

Summer Leys Nature Reserve – elusive tree sparrows

SUMMER LEYS LOCAL NATURE RESERVE

This splendid habitat is fed by Grendon Brook, an exceptionally clean flow which serves to replenish the nutrients required by birds and other animals in their food source, where stone loach and bullheads linger.

Several ponds, all accessible, enable short-range viewing of frogs and toads, at breeding time, to follow the fascinating process of spawning and its development through the crucial stages to become real live amphibians.

Waders such as the wood sandpiper and greenshank alight here on their long migrations between the north and Africa in spring and again in autumn. Watch for the fast-flying hobby in summer and winter wildfowl later in the year. The reserve is also favoured by the sleek presence of the largest colony of the common tern in the country.

Lakes and wetland are left as a result of gravel extraction, but now the machinery has moved on and another wondrous site has developed, leaving us richer because of it.

Flora and fauna add to the pleasure, where only a few years ago, this was just a couple of beanfields.

PLACES OF INTEREST
EARLS BARTON

The redeeming feature of Earls Barton must surely be the most attractive centre entirely dominated by All Saints' church on the rise, which affords a long-ranging view over the rooftops across the valley toward Whiston and Cogenhoe (pronounced Cooknoe).

The late Saxon tower of 970AD and incorporated later work, such as the typical zig-zag pattern of the stonework in the south porch, the medieval rood screen, Victorian furnishings and more recent windows, add charm to this place steeped in history.

Behind this building is an intriguing site with a very deep ditch, identified as a Norman castle-motte site.

Known at the time of Domesday Book in 1066 as Buarton(e), Countess Judith, niece of William the Conqueror, is listed as being a landowner in these parts.

In the 14th and 15th centuries, the manufacture of woollen goods was the main industry, in addition to the production of the weaving of rushes from the nearby river, into mats and baskets. Lace-making, too, was a part of the cottage enterprise and still retains local interest. Even earlier, leather came to the fore, being tanned in the village. Cobblers fashioned shoes in their own backyard workshops. A leading shoe manufacturer exists today to maintain these local trades.

Earls Barton may be reached on foot as an extended walk along the river bank, to the west on the Nene Way, right into the centre of the village.

IRCHESTER COUNTRY PARK

The country park takes its name from the nearby village and was the result of quarrying for ironstone, known formerly as Wembley Pit until the 1960s, when the land was purchased by Northamptonshire County Council and opened as a public amenity in 1971.

One outstanding feature on the perimeter is the quarry, which has been left untouched and consequently is of immense interest to visiting school parties, fossil hunters and nature lovers. The strata of the rock face is a clear indication of the former industry, where primitive diggers hacked away at the iron ore and labourers trundled wheelbarrows over planks to tip the waste, resulting in the hilly-holly terrain.

Conifers were planted on the ridges some 50 years ago, resulting in shady walks layered with pine needles. These are being systematically replaced by broadleaf native species to produce a mixed woodland for the future.

Covering 220 acres, with ponds, broad meadows and cool walks, many mammals, birds, particularly woodpeckers and small reptiles abound in this habitat.

The stone slab on the mound outside the Ranger's Office is said to be a lid from a Roman coffin discovered in the vicinity, though few may be aware of it.

Within the park, the Irchester Narrow Gauge Railway Trust have a working museum, including locomotives from the quarry era, where the keen volunteers are usually active at weekends.

WALK 12

TWYWELL HILLS AND DALES AND TWYWELL VILLAGE
Distance 3 miles
Map OS Landranger 141. 1:50 000
Grid ref: SP 945775
Nearest town – Thrapston

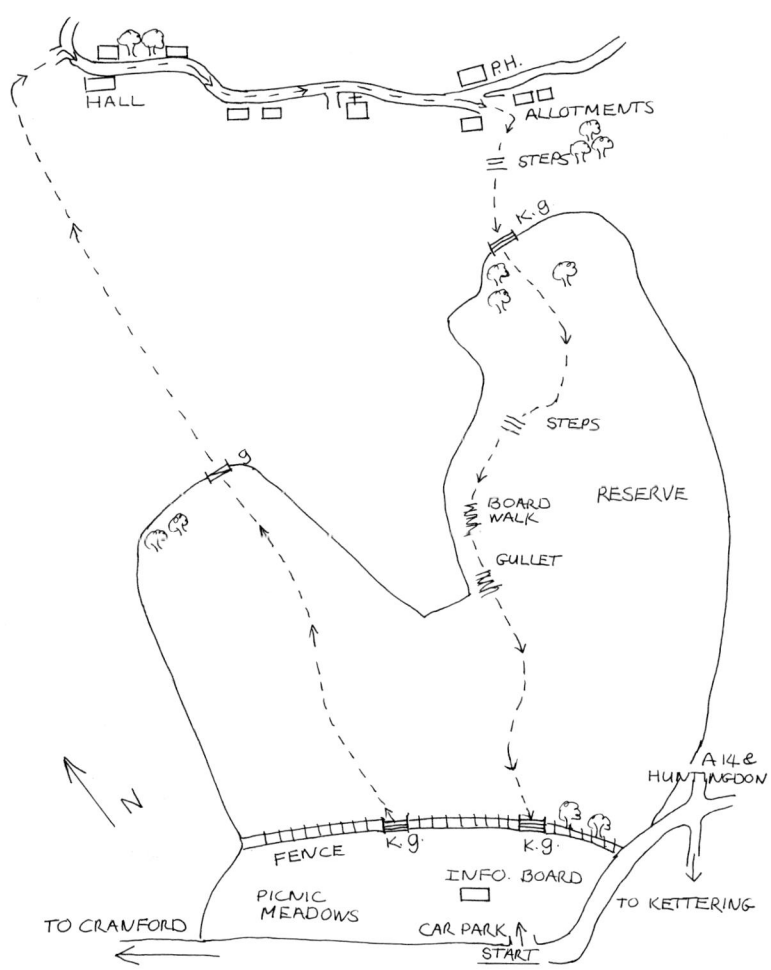

'Only a bowshot' off the dreaded A14, the gates into Twywell Hills and Dales open to a very different and absorbing world!

Here, lying between the two villages of Cranford and Twywell, linked by footpaths (although a little obscure after construction of the A14), the frantic frenzy of commercialism might be forgotten, except for the occasional hum of traffic which could impinge every now and then, but will possibly be pushed out of mind as one delves deeper into this glory of humps and hollows.

A ramble through the long rift of the gullet, an SSSI (Site of Special Scientific Interest) alone, will keep the walker entranced. The twists and turns of the path, the irregular angles of the gradients, protruding chunks of rock and the odd abandoned iron rail from the old line, is a natural delight. Sometimes lifting, then suddenly plunging, the well-defined way unfolds on differing levels.

Out of sight, no doubt a plethora of mammals and amphibians are secreted in their various hidey-holes. Insects both on and off the wing and the mysterious rustling in the bushes or what might be under that stone or in that crevice.

Twywell Hills and Dales Quarry path

The seasons bring endless changes, from the fresh green buds of spring, through the subtle hues of perfume and clouds of blossom in summer, to the glowing tones of autumn and the barrenness of winter.

If every picture tells a story, this indeed, would be a picture book to stir the senses!

WALK

On the open space next to the car park, refer to the information board for the several options available, but for the circuit described, cross the picnic meadows to the Whitestones trail ahead, an easy walk over grazing land.

Exit at the far corner where there is another map and hedgerows meet, to the bridle-way to Twywell about 3/4 mile away. Just before the village, the route turns right to meet the road on the outskirts adjacent to MacQueen House, the guiding centre.

Walk down the hill and as the street widens, the Old Friar pub stands back at the far end. On the other side, cut through a narrow lane between detached houses to the allotments, turning in by a tall hedge and fence which runs along the top of a low escarpment to a kissing-gate and steps with a handrail, by a knoll with trees.

Twywell Hills and Dales glades

Almost opposite across the field a kissing-gate leads back into the reserve, going up a sharp rise to the wide riding. First comes the wooden fingerpost, so cross here to take the next right, to veer off at the rim of the gullet and down, down, down to the bottom to tread the irresistable trail, though not recommended for the faint-hearted or less agile. Boardwalks are well-placed here and there to enable access over sometimes muddy patches (If this trail is deemed too arduous, keep straight on to ultimately gain the meadows).

At the junction with Whitestones, bear left on either of the undulating paths to return to start.

TWYWELL HILLS AND DALES RESERVE

Yet another reserve, this one of 135 acres, comprising two disused ironstone quarries abandoned since 1957 and 1959, where iron ore was dug and transported by trucks and rail system to the former Islip furnaces up the road toward Thrapston.

The mix of terrain should suit everyone, as there are gradual grassland slopes for the quiet types and rocky gorges for those who seek exploration.

There is an excellent leaflet *'Pig Iron and Old Men'* issued by the Rockingham Trust and highly recommended for the full story of men and machines in those early dangerous throes of mining.

The site is a partnership between The Rockingham Forest, The Wildfowl and Woodland Trusts and East Northamptonshire Council, supported by the Heritage Lottery Fund and the Countryside Commission.

PLACES OF INTEREST

BOUGHTON HOUSE

The grand mansion, Boughton House, is romantically set in harmonious parkland and is the Northamptonshire home of the Duke of Buccleuch and Queensbury.

The classical lines of the façade suggest a French chateau, yet inside, superb collections of art, furniture, tapestries and silver are amassed, as well as an armoury.

Outwardly, the complexity of a house with 12 entrances, 7 courtyards, 52 chimneystacks and 365 windows, is overwhelming, crowned by 1 1/4 acres of Collyweston roof tiles.

Though no longer viable, the water-gardens were at one time an important feature. The rides and avenue of elm trees were laid out by John the Planter, an enterprising landowner, who had other estates beside this one. Unfortunately the elms were diminished years later by disease, though the lines of mature limes have mostly survived.

John married Mary Churchill, a daughter of the Duke of Marlborough in 1705 and was to succeed his own father, Ralph Montagu in 1709. There is much to see and enjoy here, where sensitive modern methods have enhanced this magnificent estate.

GRAFTON UNDERWOOD

Grafton Underwood is perhaps remembered for the sudden influx of the American Forces during the Second World War.

All around this tranquil countryside, sprawling airfields were hurriedly constructed to accommodate ponderous bombers and their support crews, who frequently flew over enemy territory. It also earned the distinction of being the field from which the first and last bombing raids of the war departed. Some planes returned battered and burned, whilst others were lost never to return.

In St. James' church, a glorious, explicit stained glass window, is dedicated to the memory of 1,579 members of the Eighth Airforce who gave their lives to the cause.

A fine granite memorial on the roadside between Grafton Underwood and Geddington, is to honour the 384th Bombardment Group (heavy) who served there the longest.

PLACES OF INTEREST

Anglian Water, The Lodge, Holcot. Off A508 Northampton to Market Harborough or off A43 Northampton to Kettering. 01604 781552. Open all year.

Boughton House. Three miles north of Kettering on A43, follow signs through Geddington village. 01536 417255. Park open daily May – September. House open August 2pm – 4.30pm.

Brixworth Country Park. Off roundabout A508 Northampton to Market Harborough near Brixworth village. 01604 883920. Open daily. Ranger service.

Canal Museum, Stoke Bruerne, Towcester. Off A508 south of Northampton. 01604 862229. Open summer 10 – 5. Winter 10 – 4. Closed Christmas Day and Boxing Day.

Earls Barton Museum of Local Life, Jeyes the Chemist, The Square, Earls Barton.

East Carlton Countryside Park. On A427 between Corby and Market Harborough. 01536 770977. Open daylight hours all year. Ranger Service.

Forest Enterprise (Forestry Commission) Top Lodge, Fineshade, near Corby. NN17 3BB. 01780 444394. Office hours.

Irchester Country Park, Gypsy Lane, Irchester. Off A509 Wellingborough to Milton Keynes. 01933 276866. Open all year. Ranger service.

Irchester Narrow Gauge Railway Trust, Irchester Country Park, Gypsy Lane, Irchester. Open Sundays and Bank Holidays.

Kirby Hall, Deene, near Corby. Off A43 four miles north-east of Corby on unclassified road. 01536 203230. April – October 10 – 6. Winter week-ends 10 – 4. Closed Christmas and New Year. English Heritage.

Lamport Hall, near Northampton, NN6 9HD. On A508 equidistant between Northampton and Market Harborough. 01604 686272. Limited opening Easter – September.

Lyveden New Bield, Custodian, New Bield Cottages, Oundle, PE8 5AT. 01832 205358. Daylight hours. National Trust.

National Dragonfly BioMuseum, Ashton Mill, near Oundle, PE8 5LZ. Off A605 roundabout at Oundle. 01832 272427. Open week-ends and Bank Holidays mid-June to mid-October 10.30 – 5. Also Dragonfly Sanctuary close by.

Northampton and Lamport Railway, Pitsford and Brampton Station, Pitsford Road, Chapel Brampton, NN6 8BA. Off A508 just north of Northampton. 01604 847318. Open Sundays and Bank Holidays.

Priest's House, Easton-on-the-Hill, near Stamford, two miles south-west of Stamford A508. Appointment only to view 01780 762619.

Rockingham Castle, Rockingham. Two miles north of Corby on A6003. 01536 770240. Limited opening April – October. Thursdays and Sundays.
Rockingham Forest Trust, Drill Hall House, Benefield Road, Oundle, PE8 4EY. 01832 274278. Office hours.

Southwick Hall, Southwick, near Oundle, PE8 5BL. Three miles north-west of Oundle. 01832 274064. Open Sundays, Mondays and Bank Holidays 2 – 5, Easter – August and some Wednesdays.

Sulgrave Manor, near Banbury, Oxon, OX17 2SD. Off B425 Northampton to Banbury. Seven miles north-east of Banbury. Open daily except Wednesdays April – October and some winter week-ends. 01295 760205.

Towcester Racecourse, Easton Neston, Towcester, NN12 7HS. One mile south-east of Towcester on A5 and ten miles from Northampton. 01327 353414.

West Lodge Rural Centre, near Desborough. Off A6 Kettering to Leicester. Open daily March – October and beyond 10 – 5. 01536 760552.

TOURIST INFORMATION CENTRES

BRACKLEY

Tourist Information Centre
2 Bridge Street
Brackley
Northamptonshire
NN13 7EP
Tel: 01280 700111
Fax: 01280 700157

CORBY

Tourist Information Centre
Festival Hall
George Street
Corby
Northamptonshire
NN17 1QB
Tel: 01536 407507
Fax: 01536 403748

DAVENTRY

Tourist Information Centre
Moot Hall
Market Square
Daventry
Northamptonshire
NN11 4BH
Tel: 01327 300277
Fax:01327 876684

KETTERING

Tourist Information Centre
The Coach House
Sheep Street
Kettering
NN16 0AN
Tel: 01536 410266
Fax: 01536 534370

NORTHAMPTON

Mr Grant's House
St. Giles' Square
Northampton
NN1 1DA
Tel: 01604 622677
Fax: 01604 604180
Email: tic@northampton.gov.uk

OUNDLE

Tourist Information Centre
14 West Street
Oundle
Northamptonshire
PE8 4EF
Tel: 01832 274333
Fax: 01832 274333
Email: oundletic@east-northamptonshire.gov.uk

WELLINGBOROUGH

Tourist Information Centre
Pebble Lane
Wellingborough
Northamptonshire
NN8 1AS
Tel: 01933 276412
Fax: 01933 442060